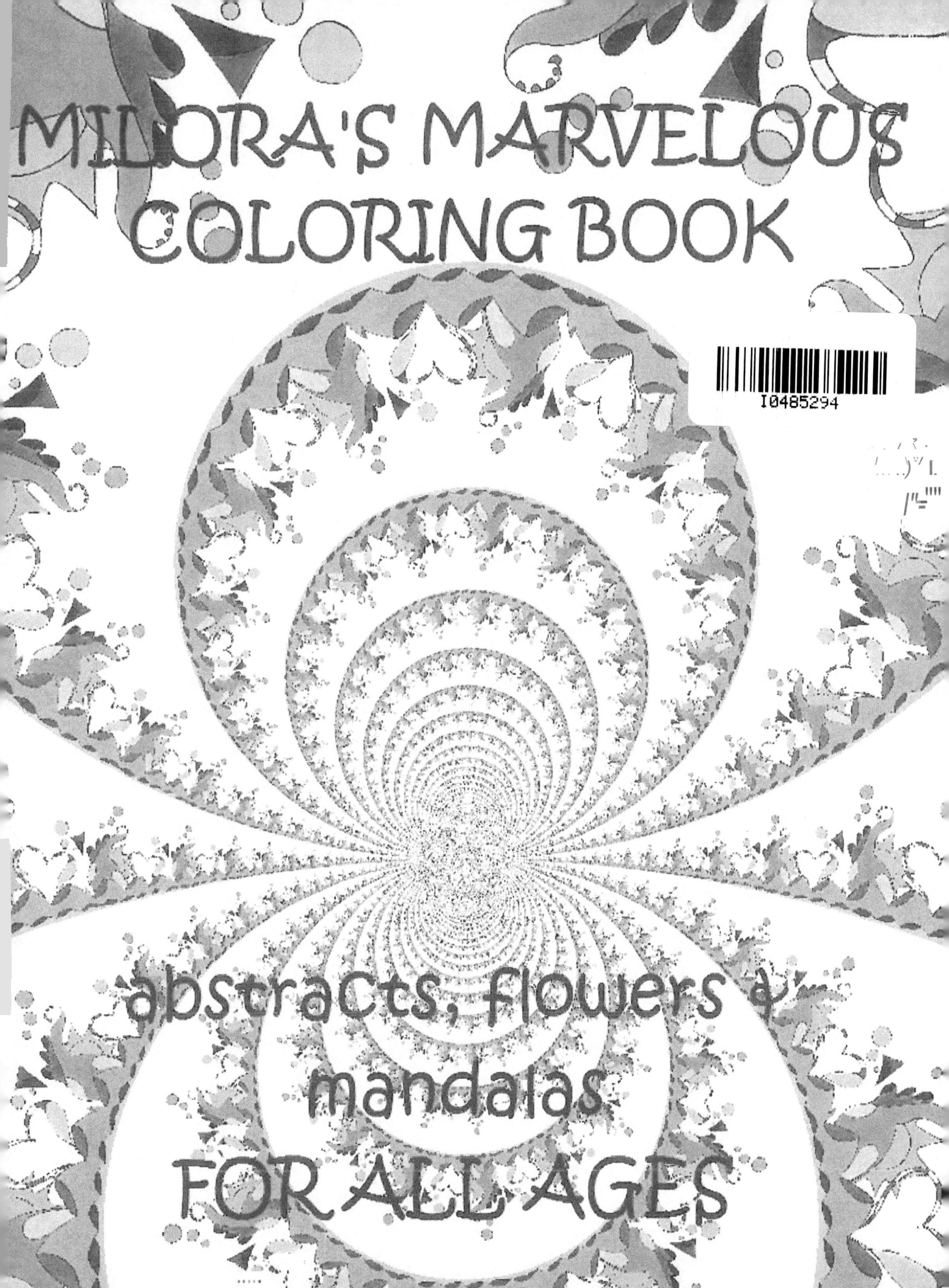

MILORA'S MARVELOUS COLORING BOOK

abstracts, flowers & mandalas

FOR ALL AGES

Printed in the United States of America

First Printing: December 2015
MIDEJA, L.L.C

ISBN # - 10: 1515324052

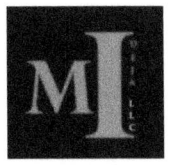

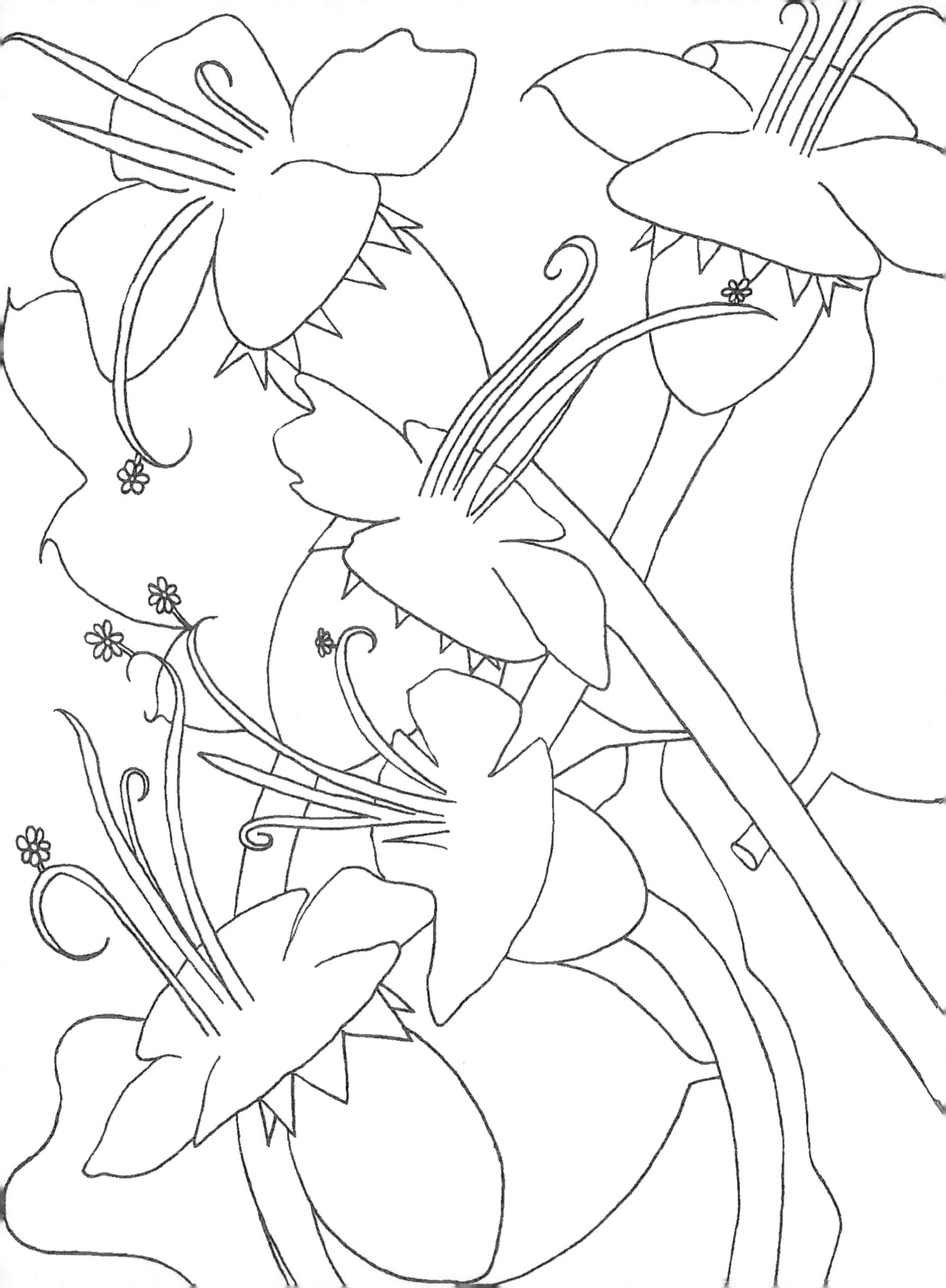

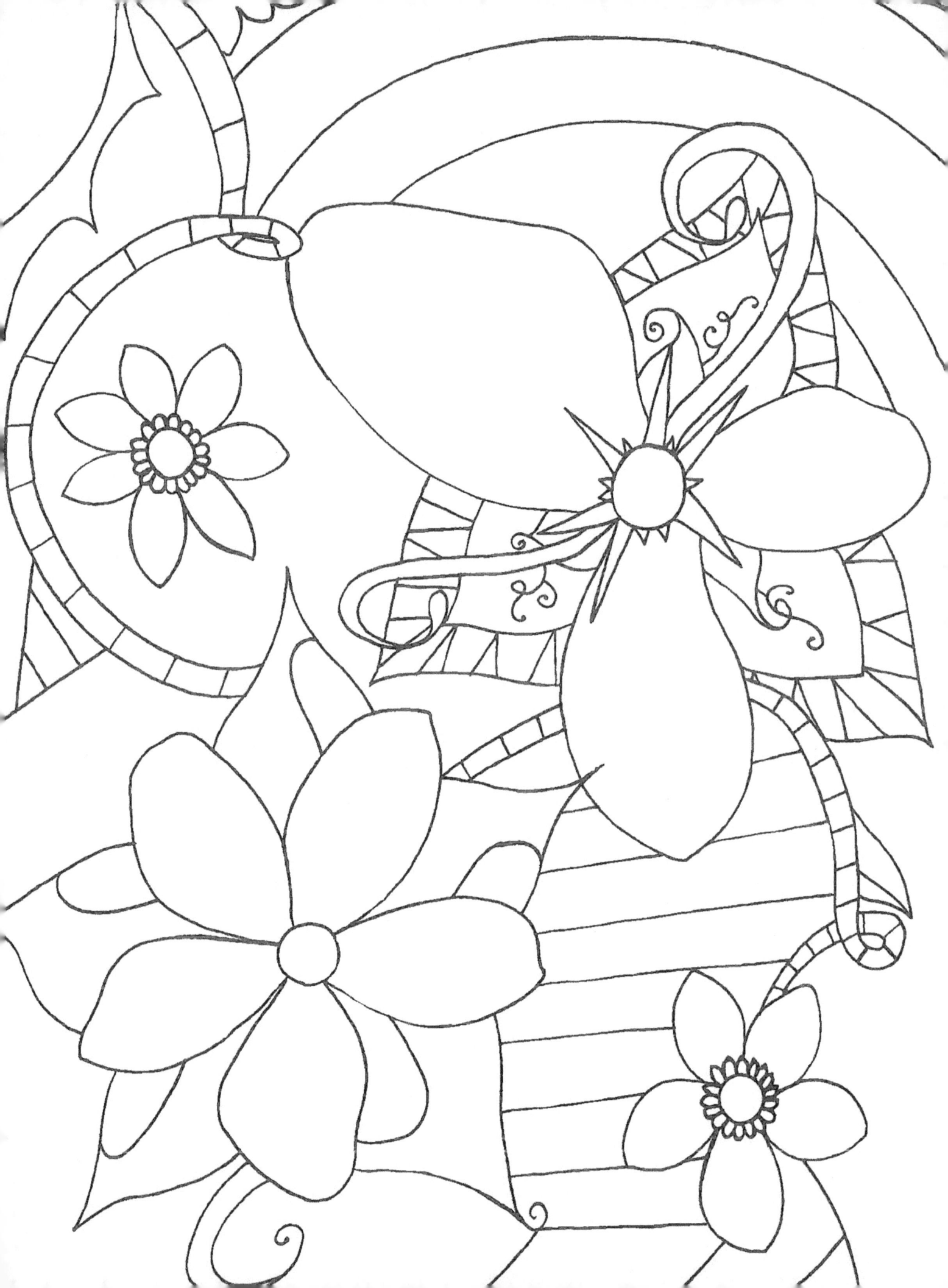

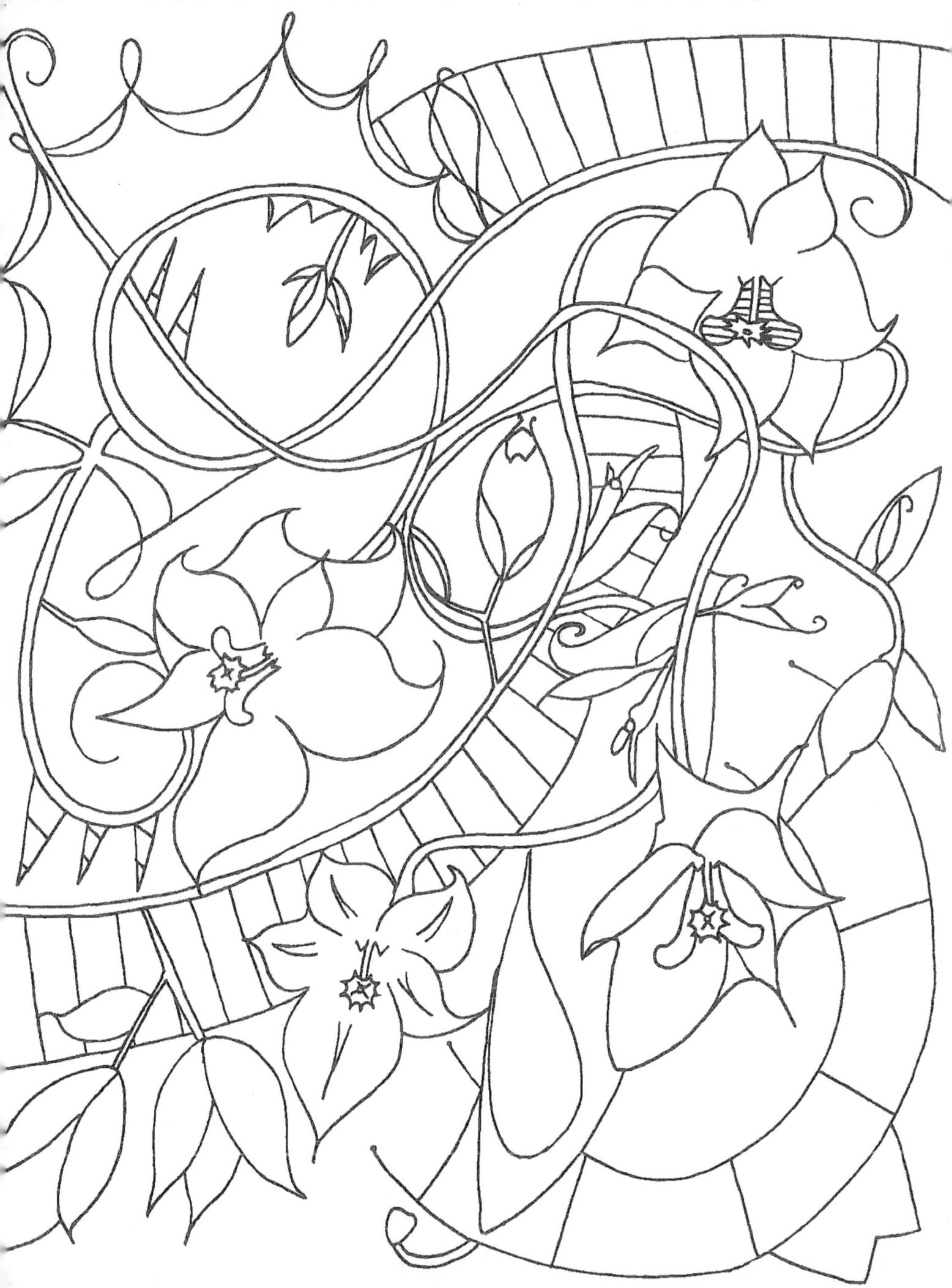

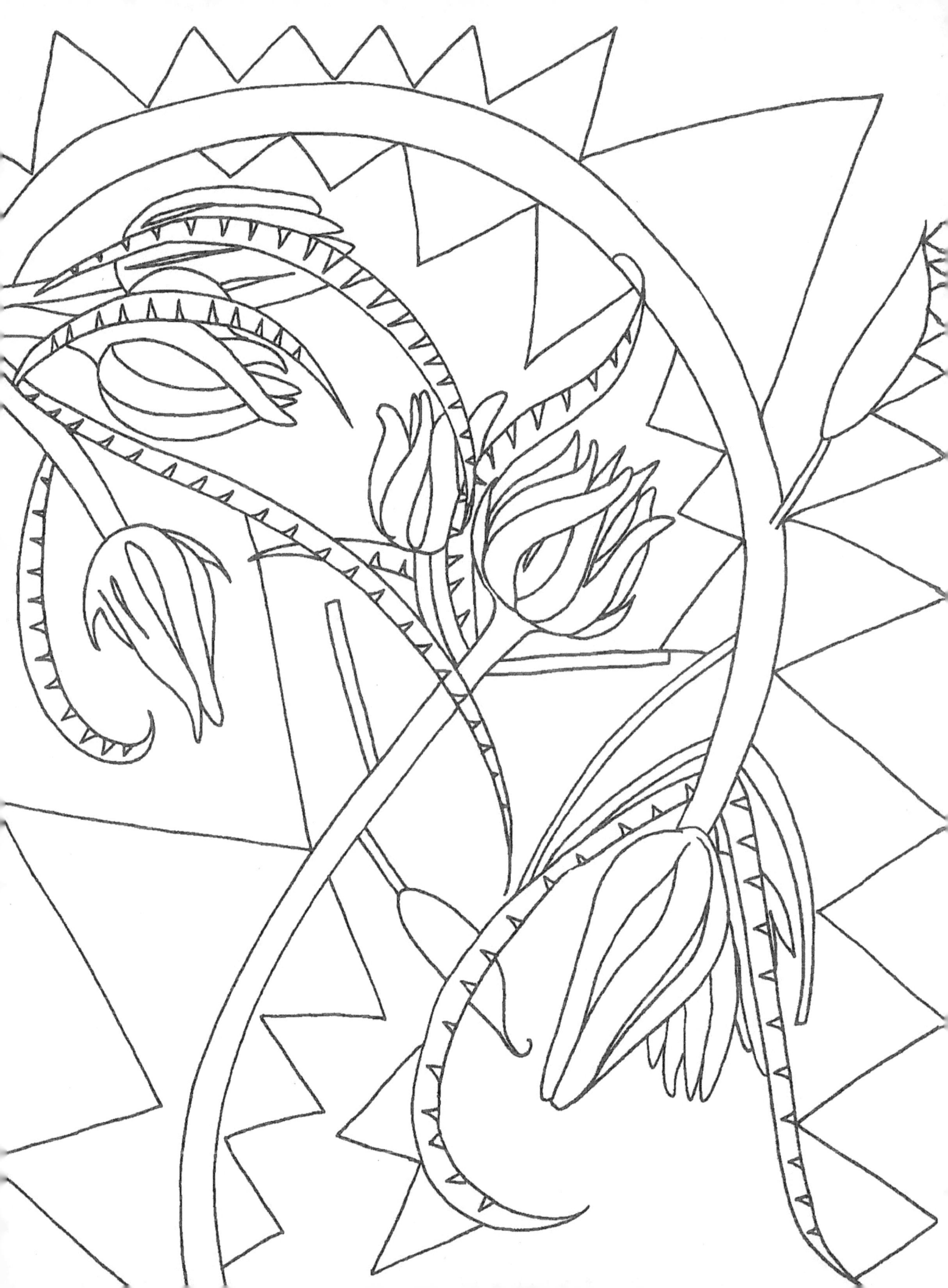

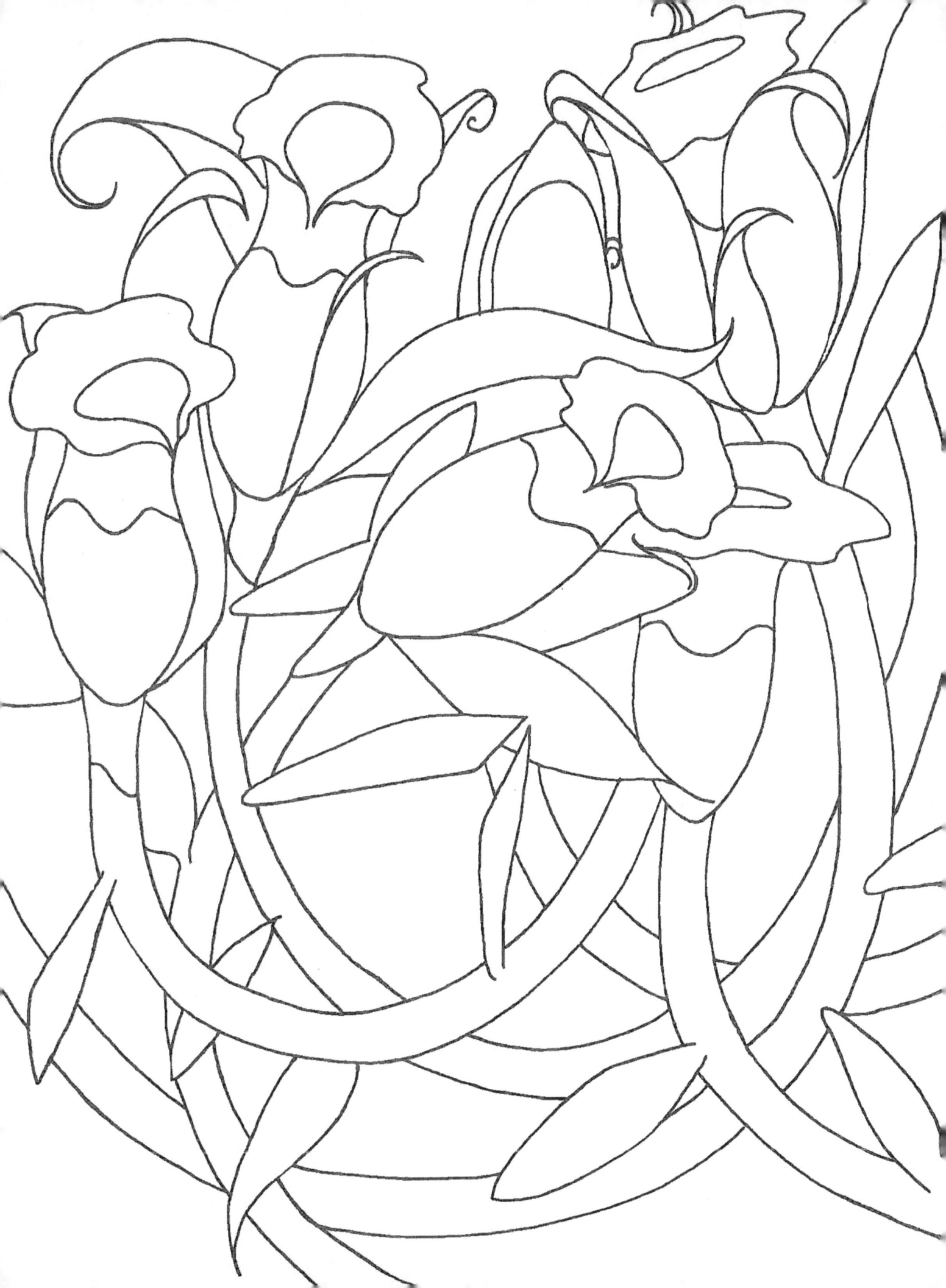

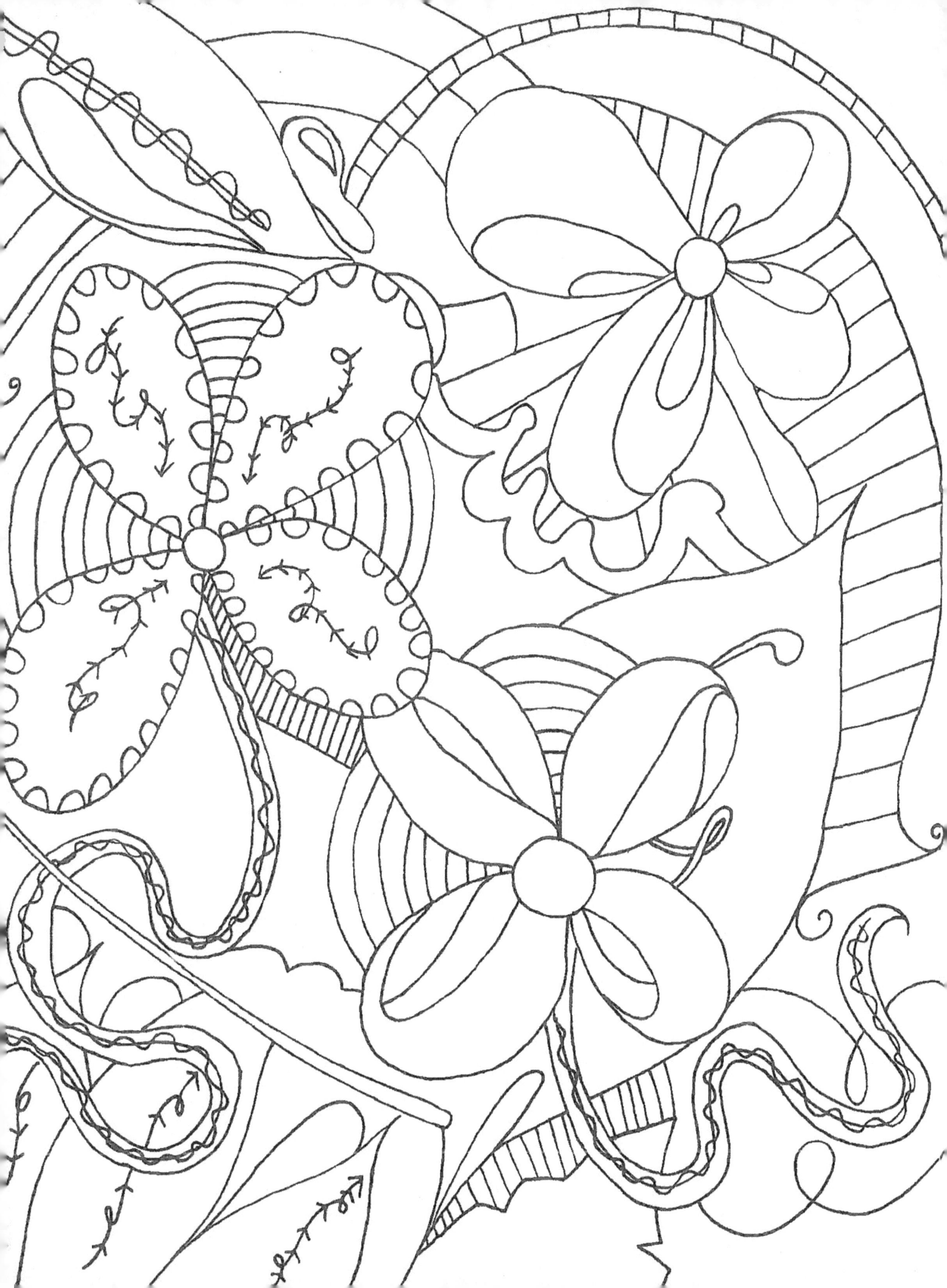

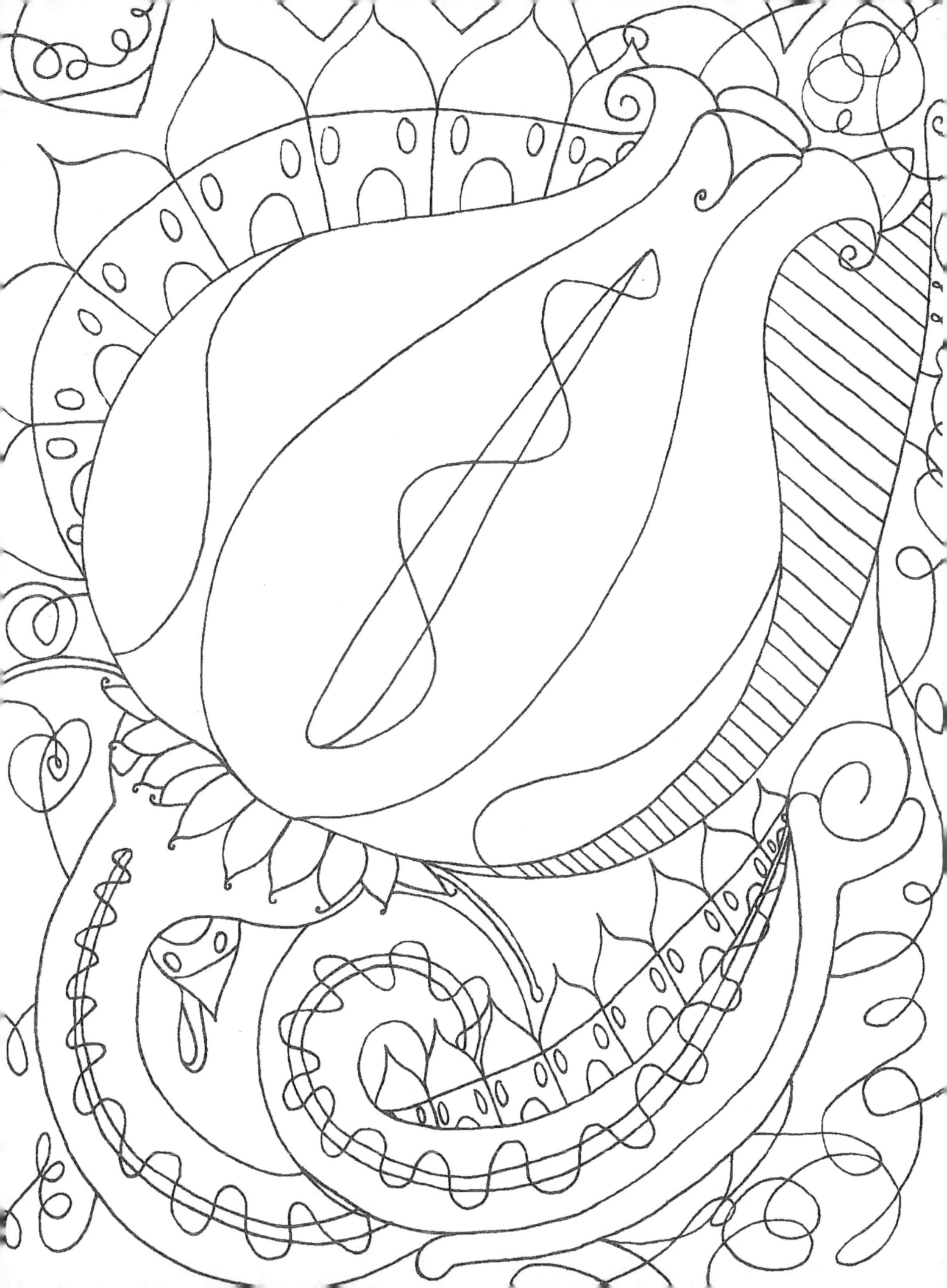

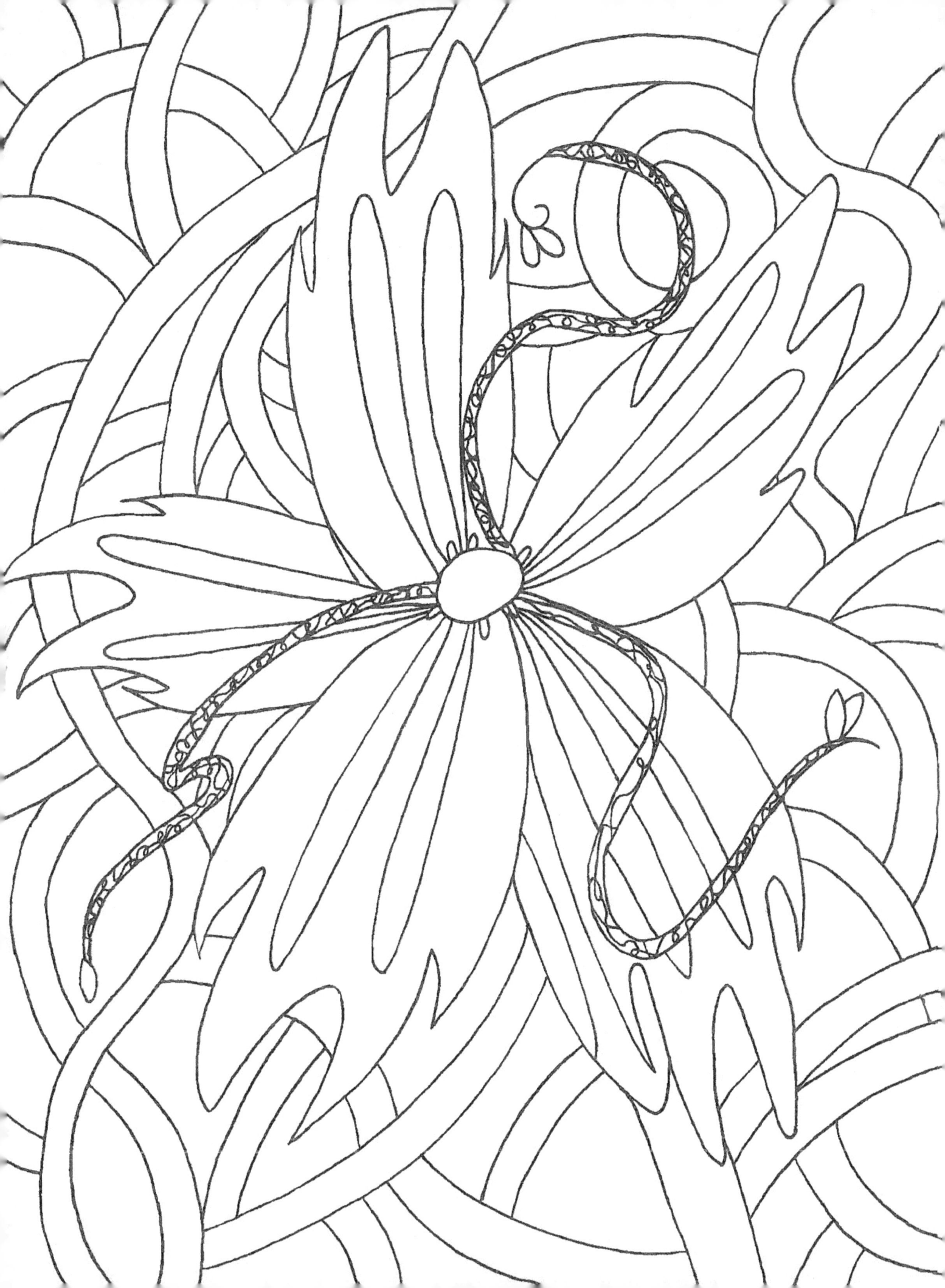

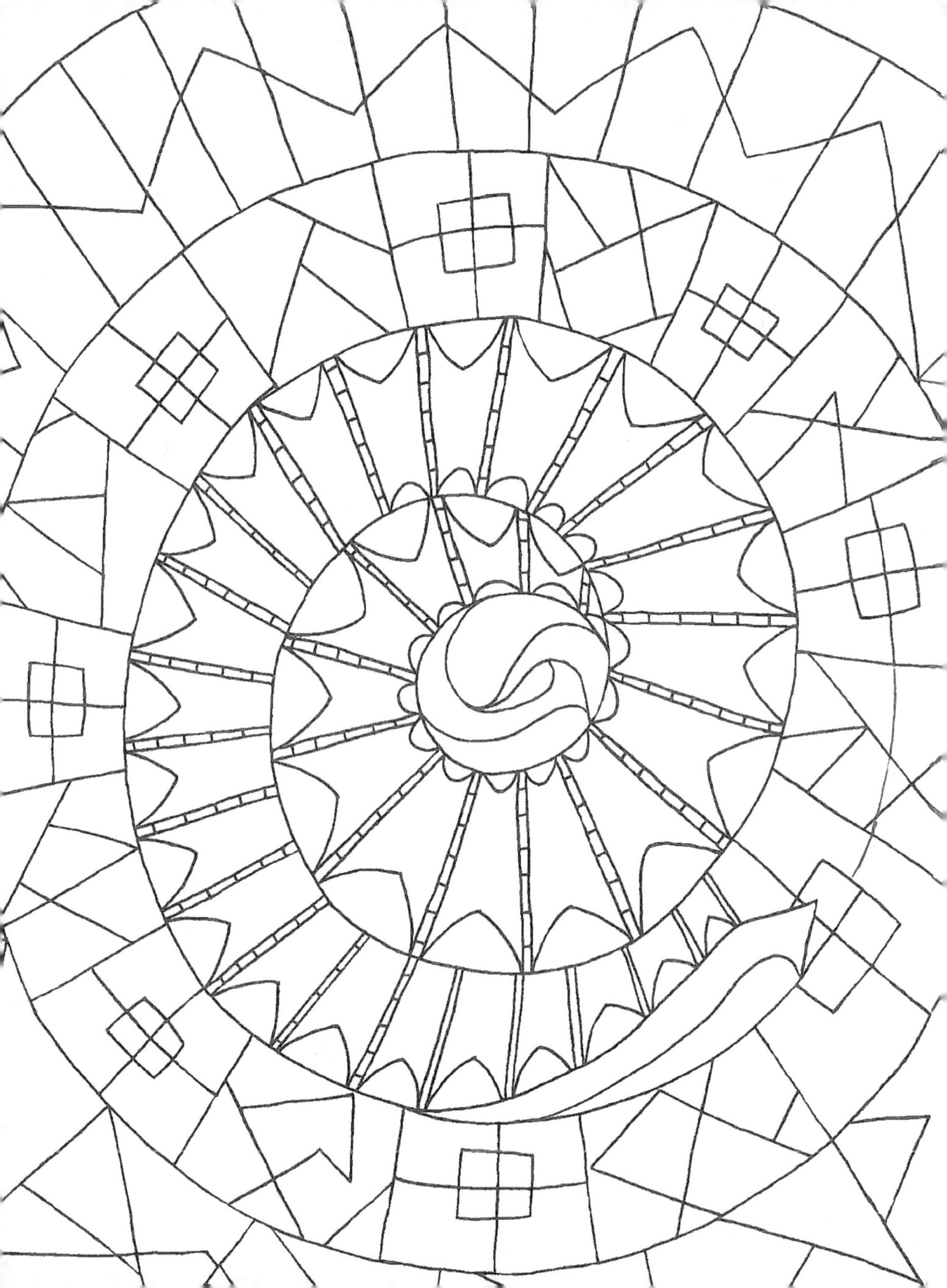

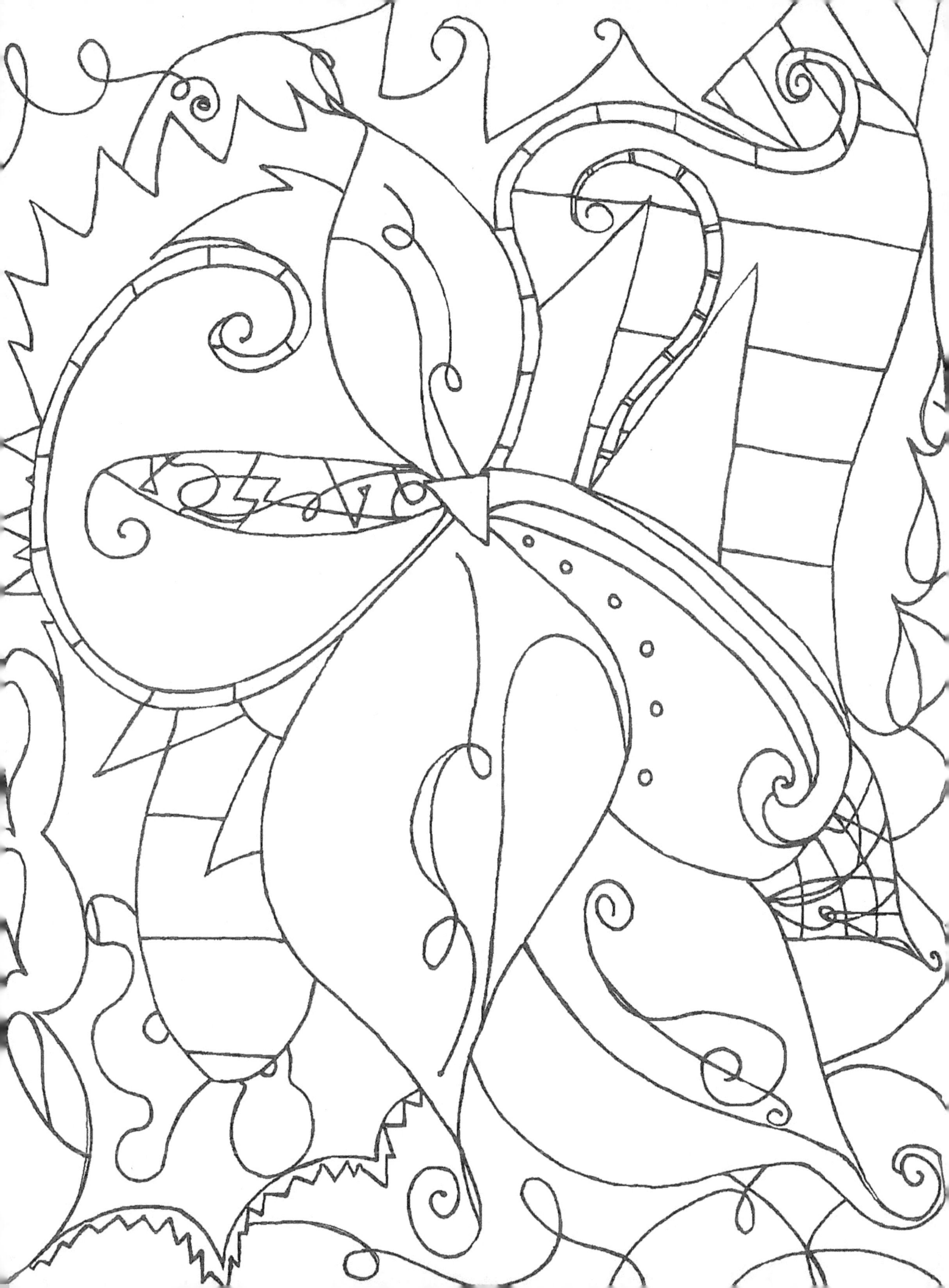

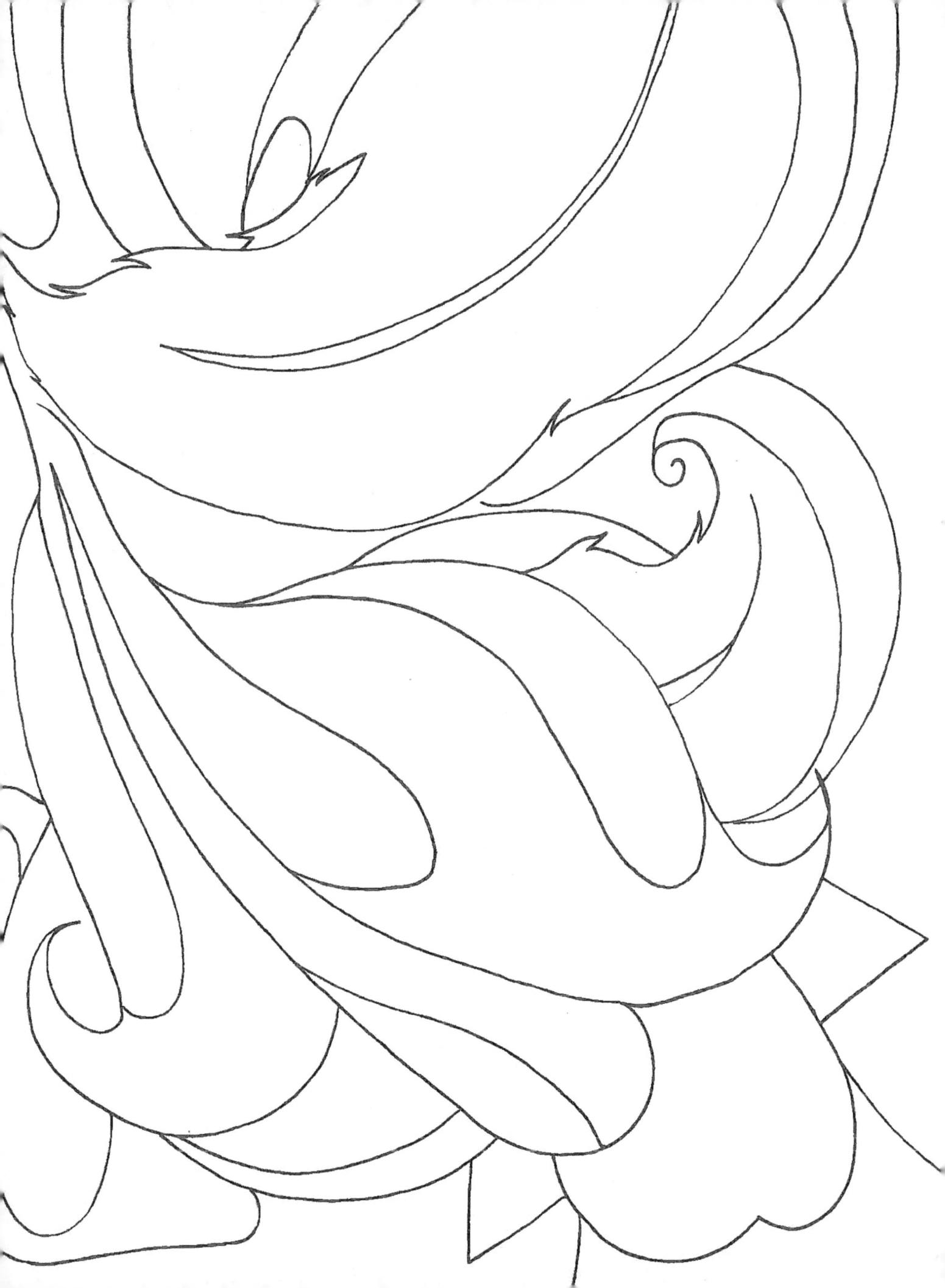

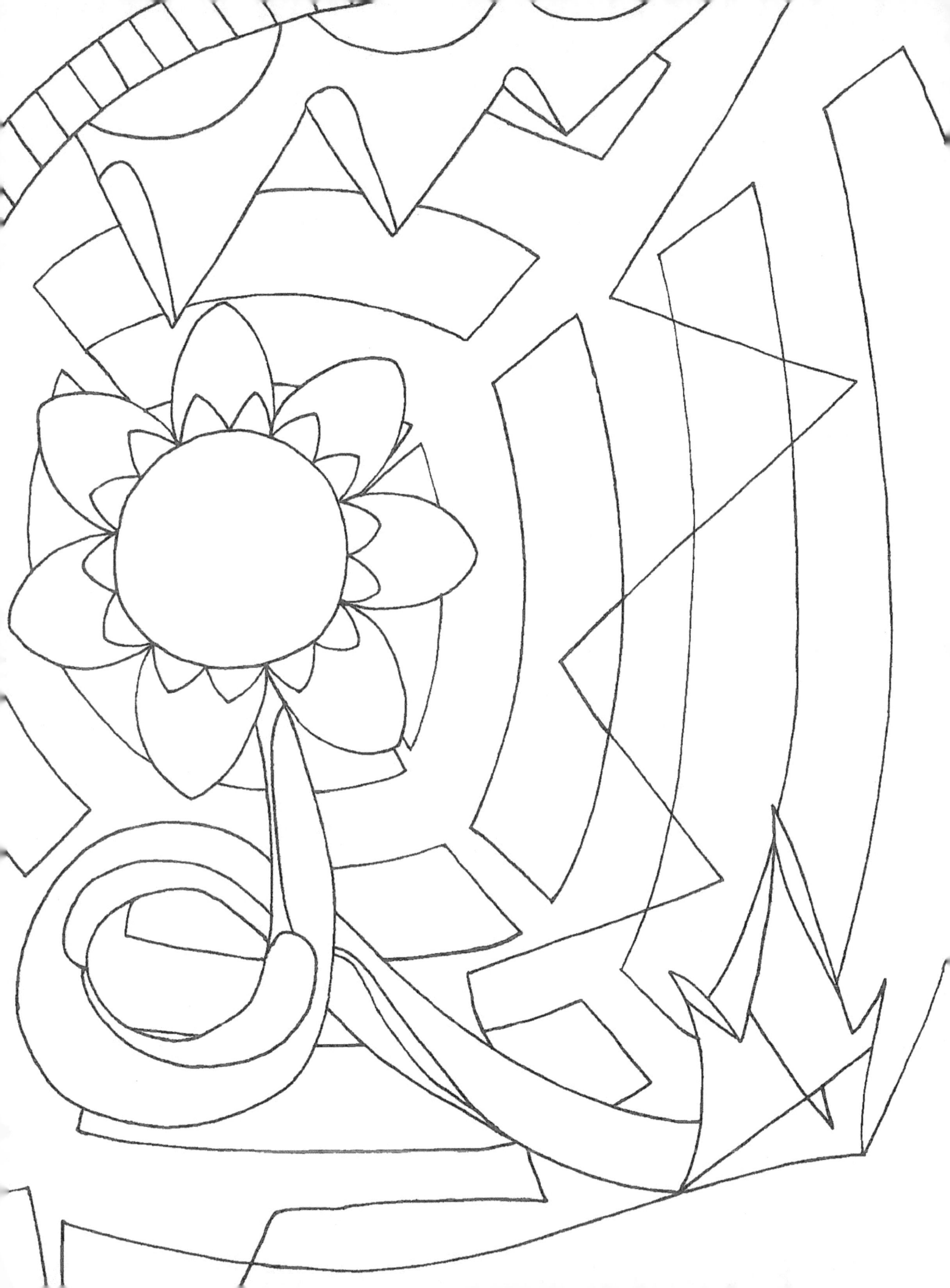

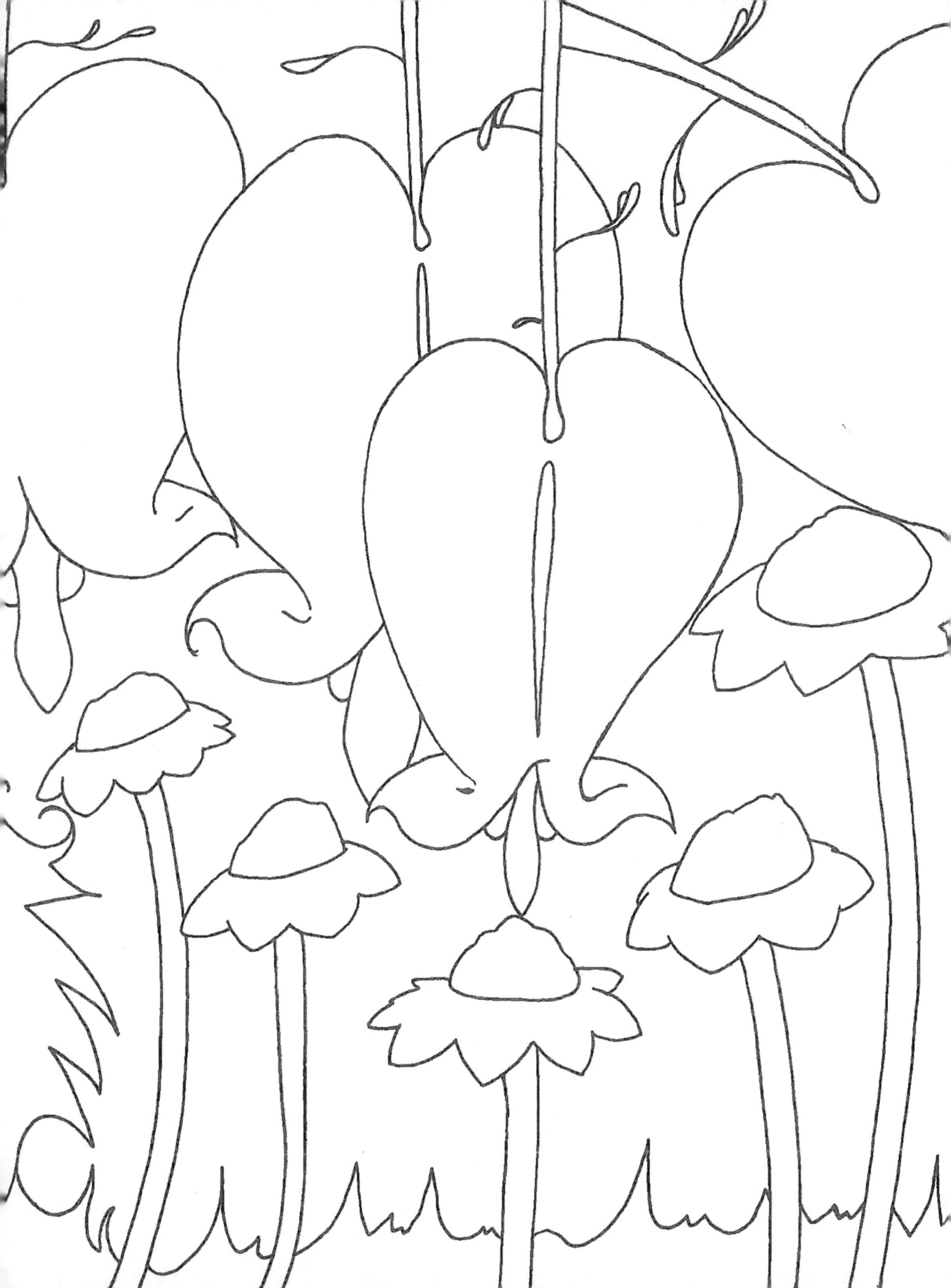

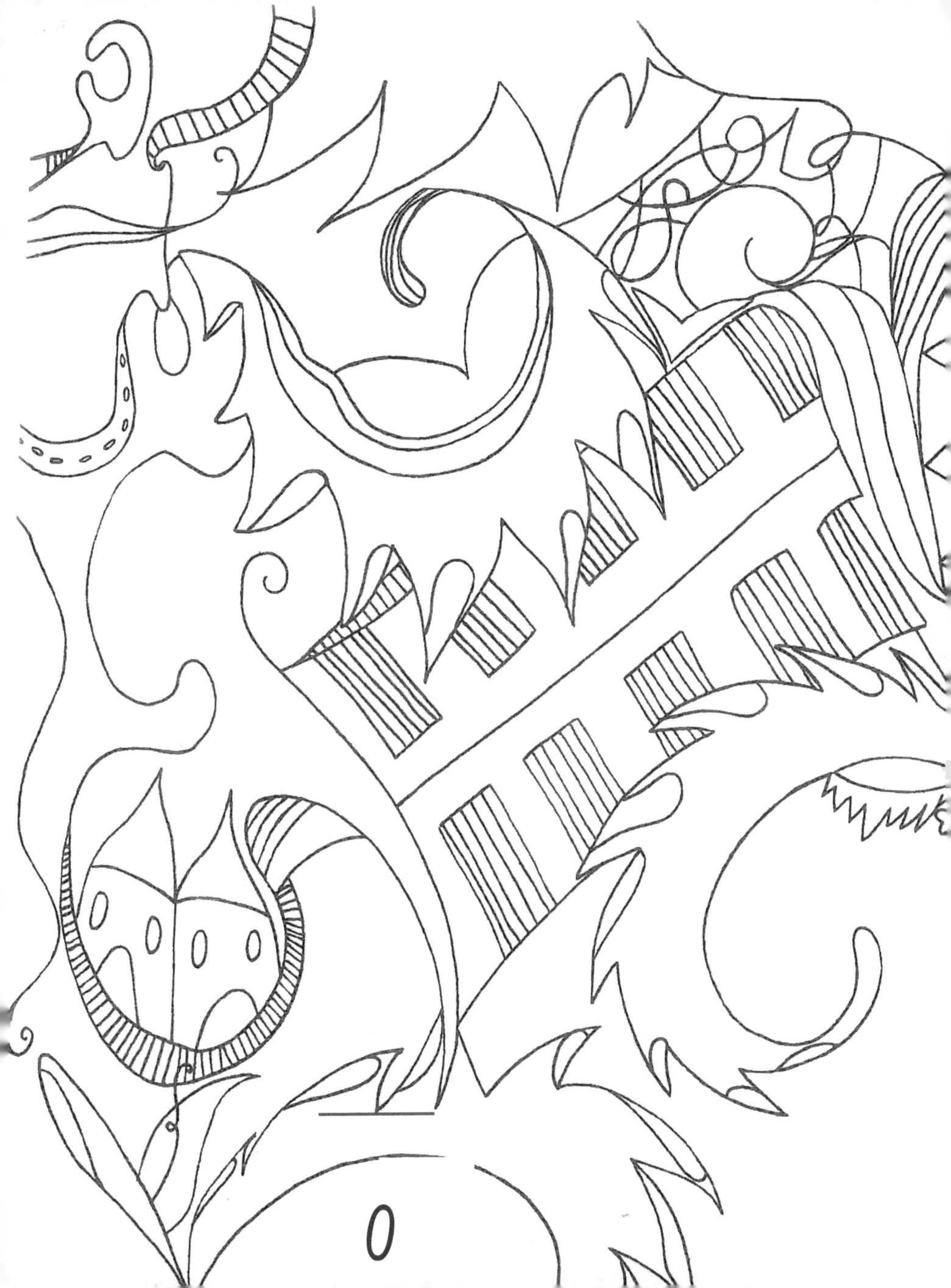

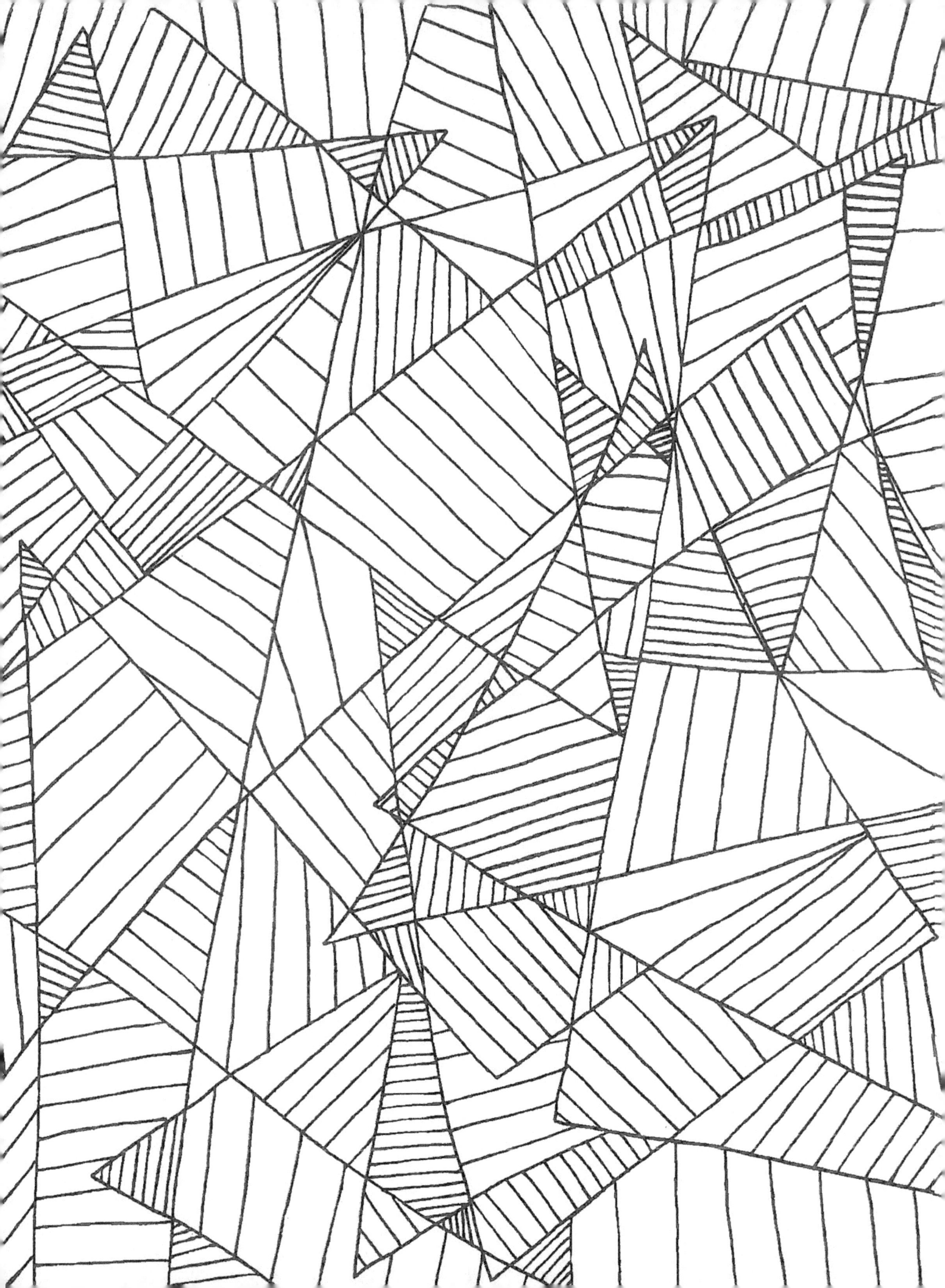

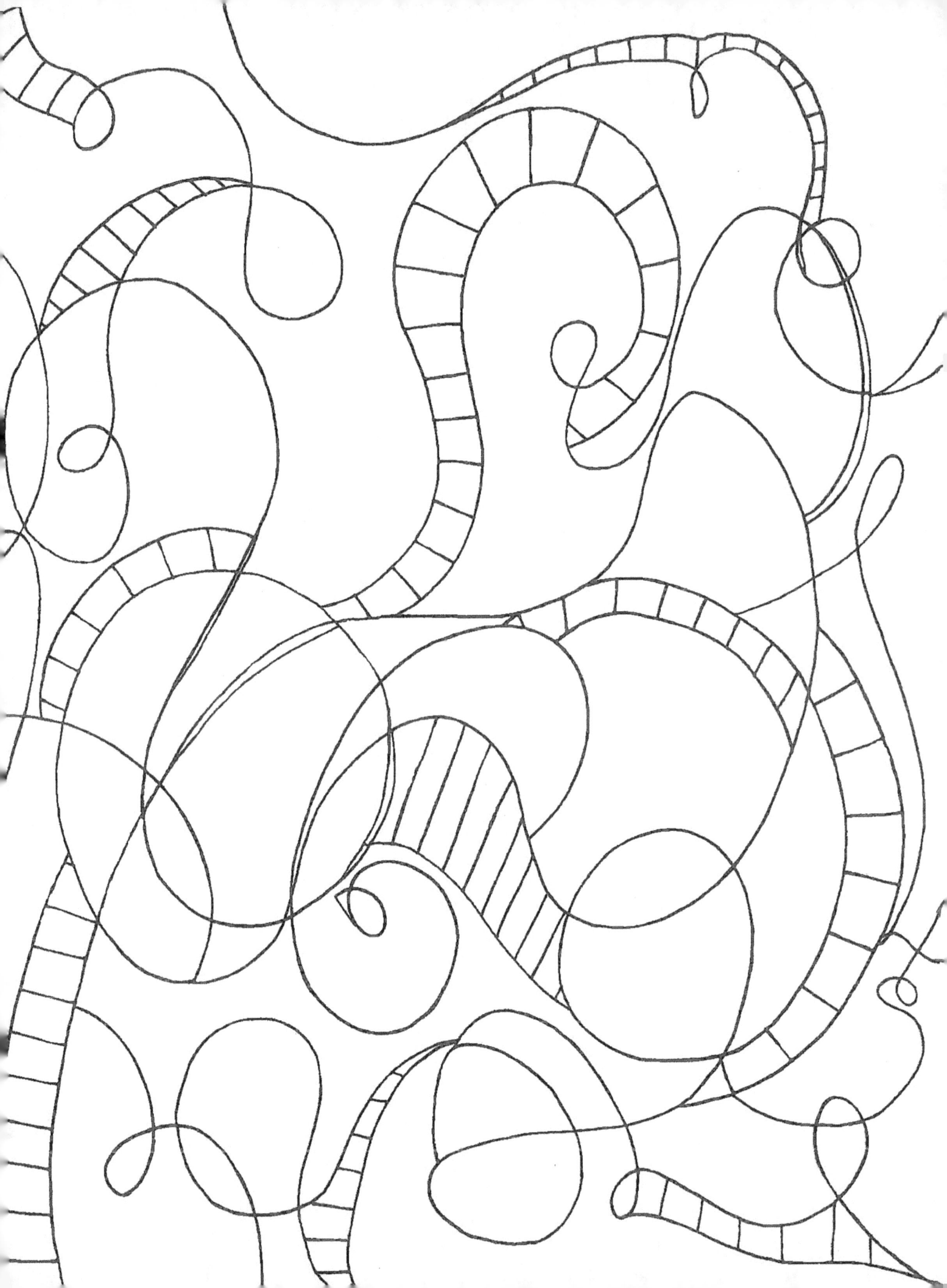

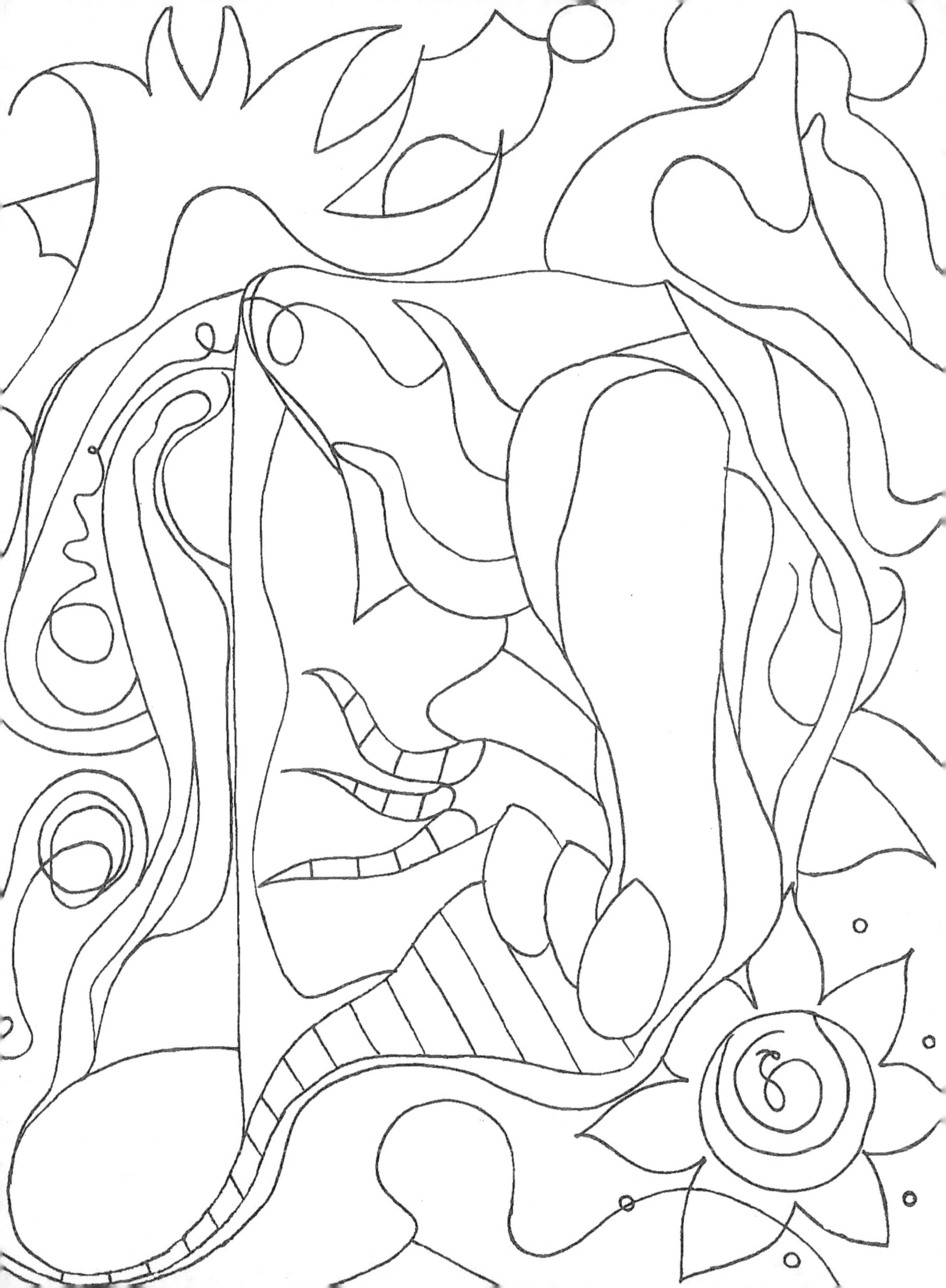

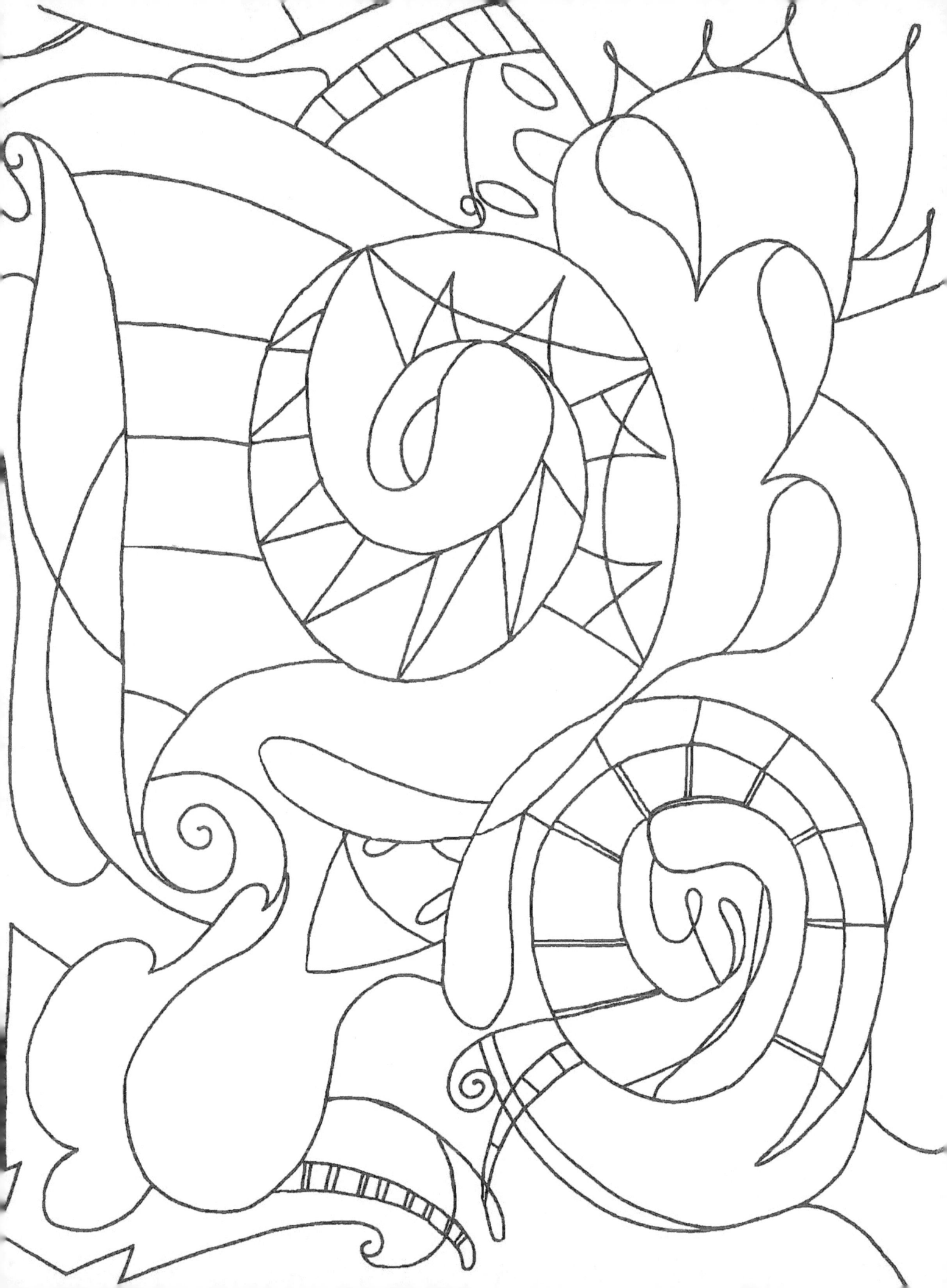

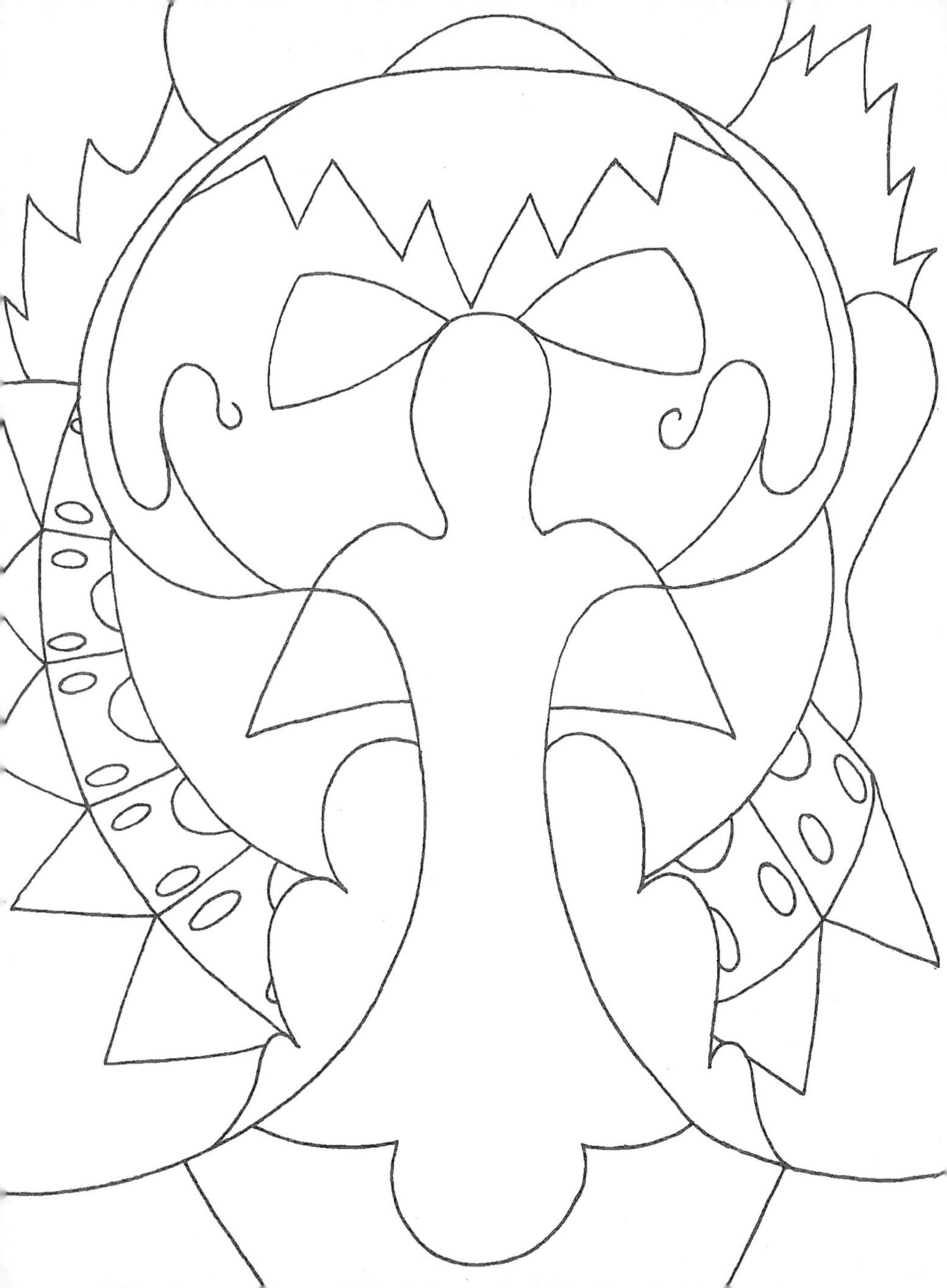

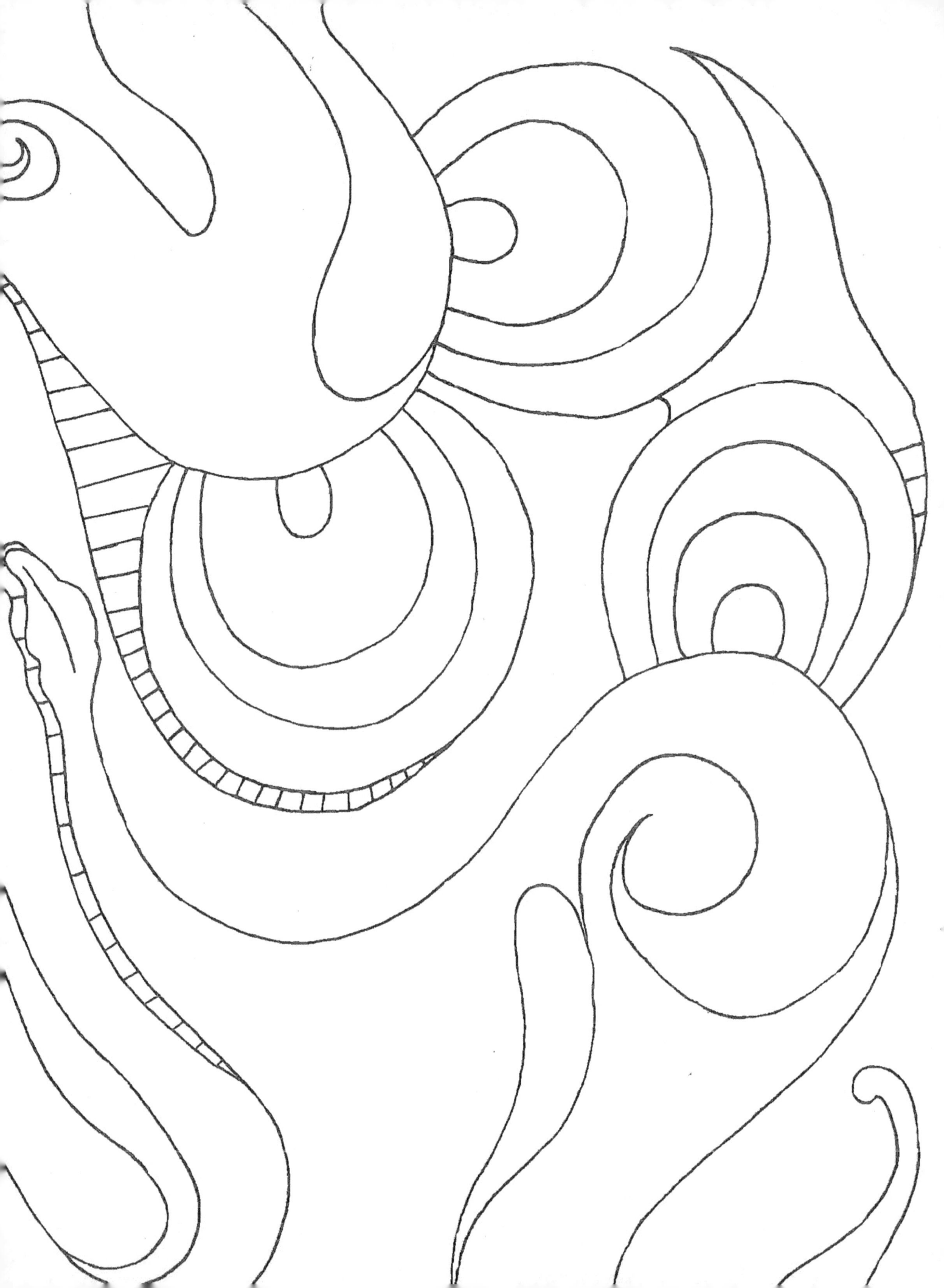

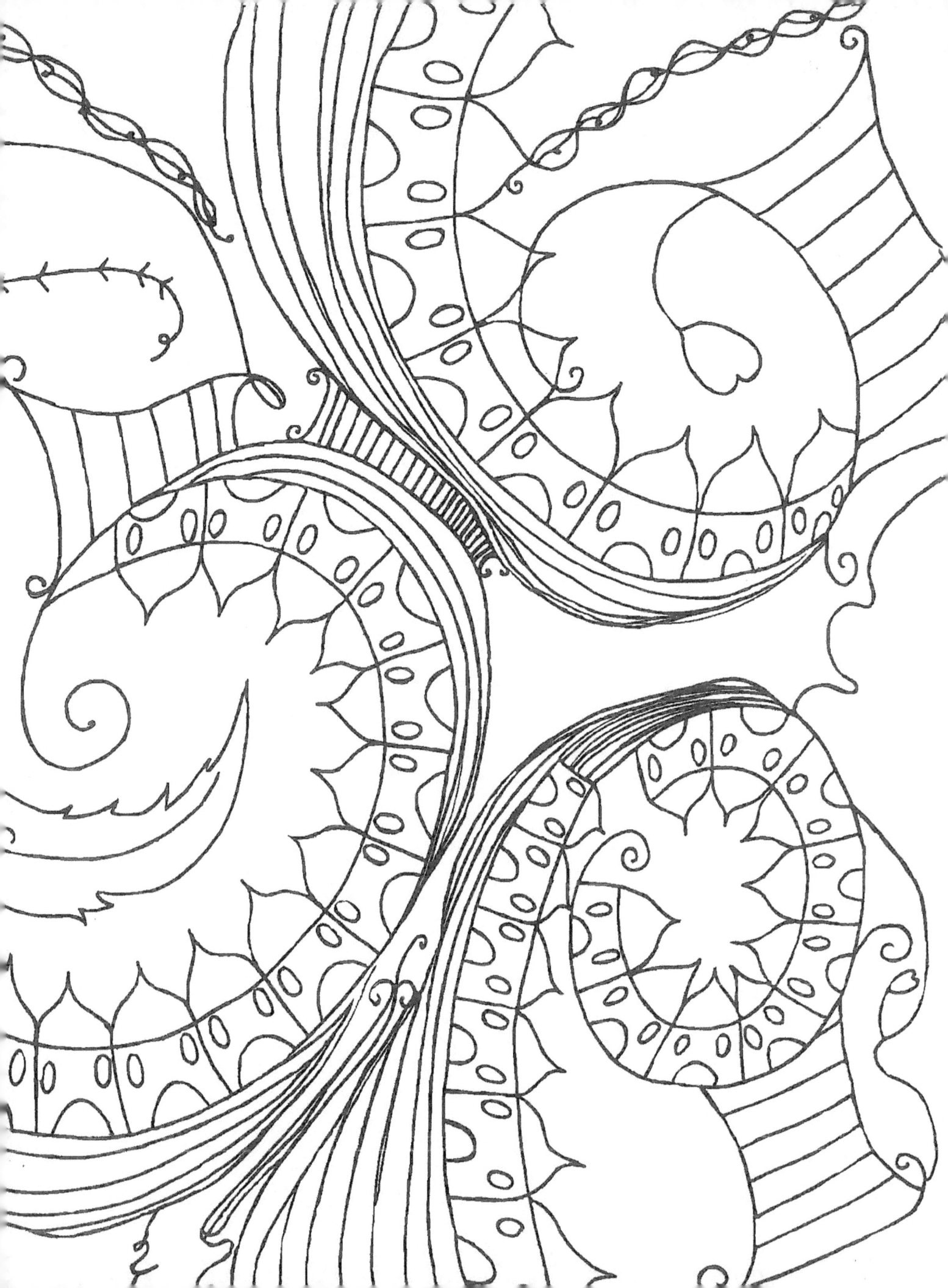

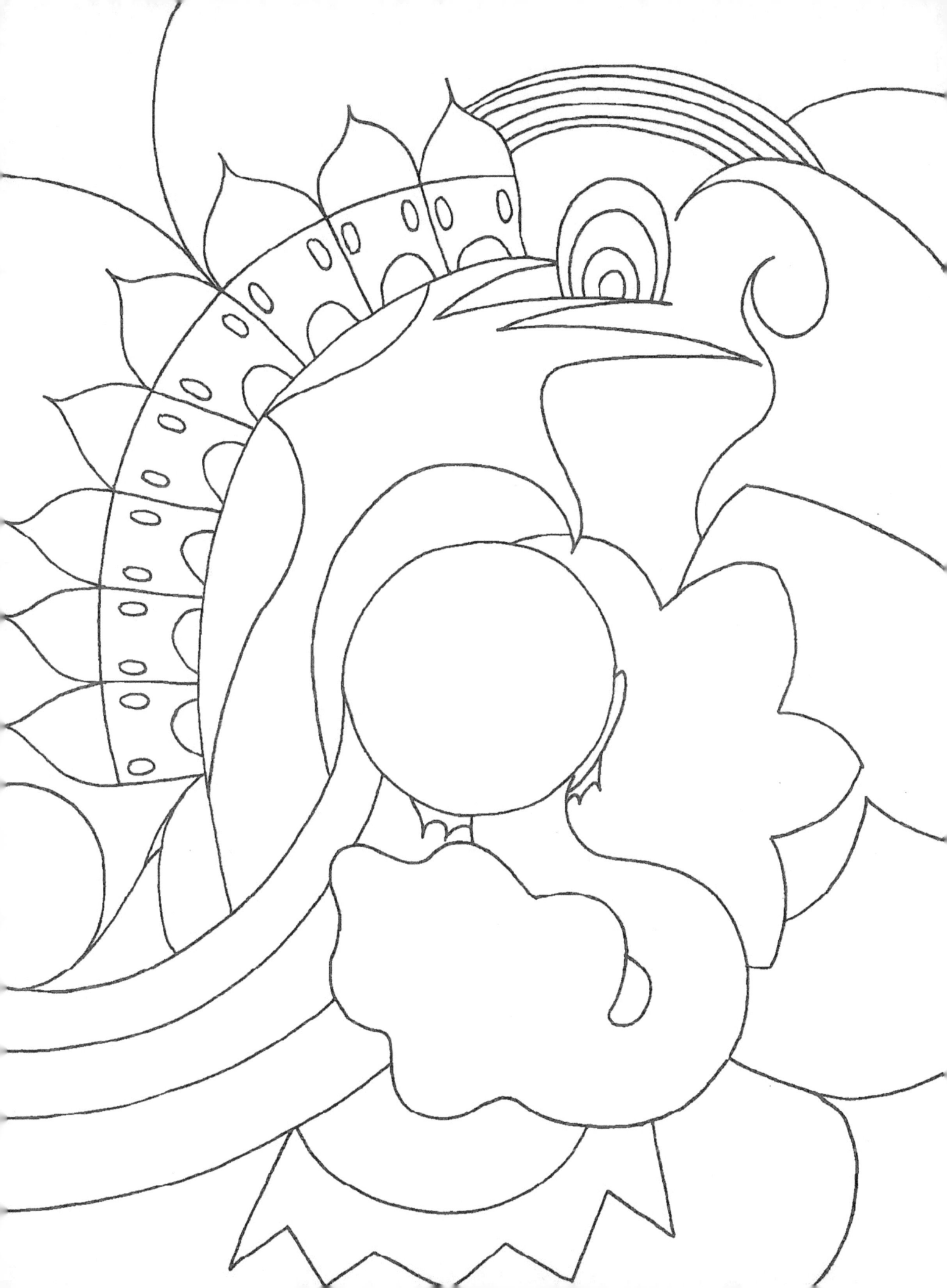

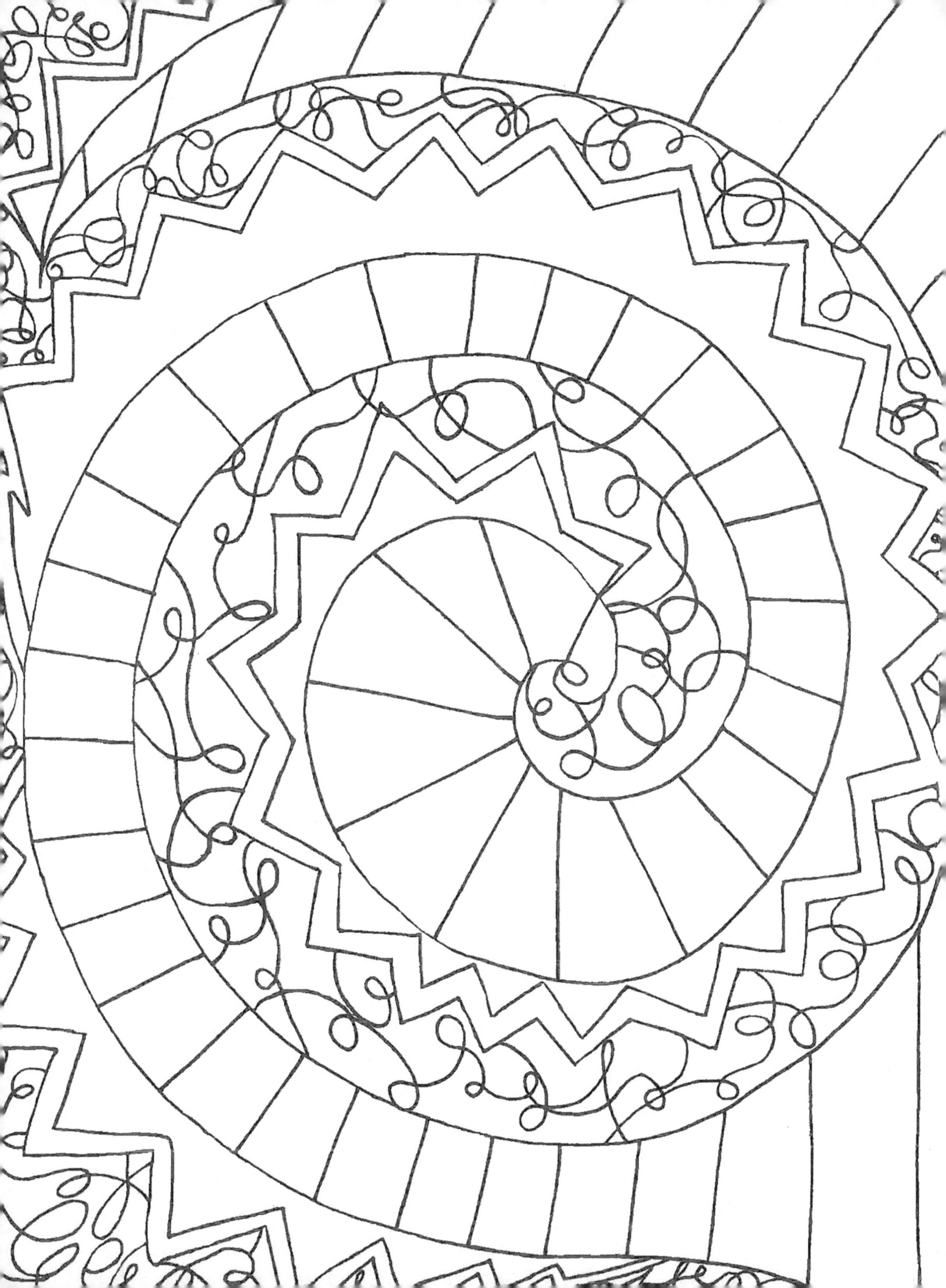

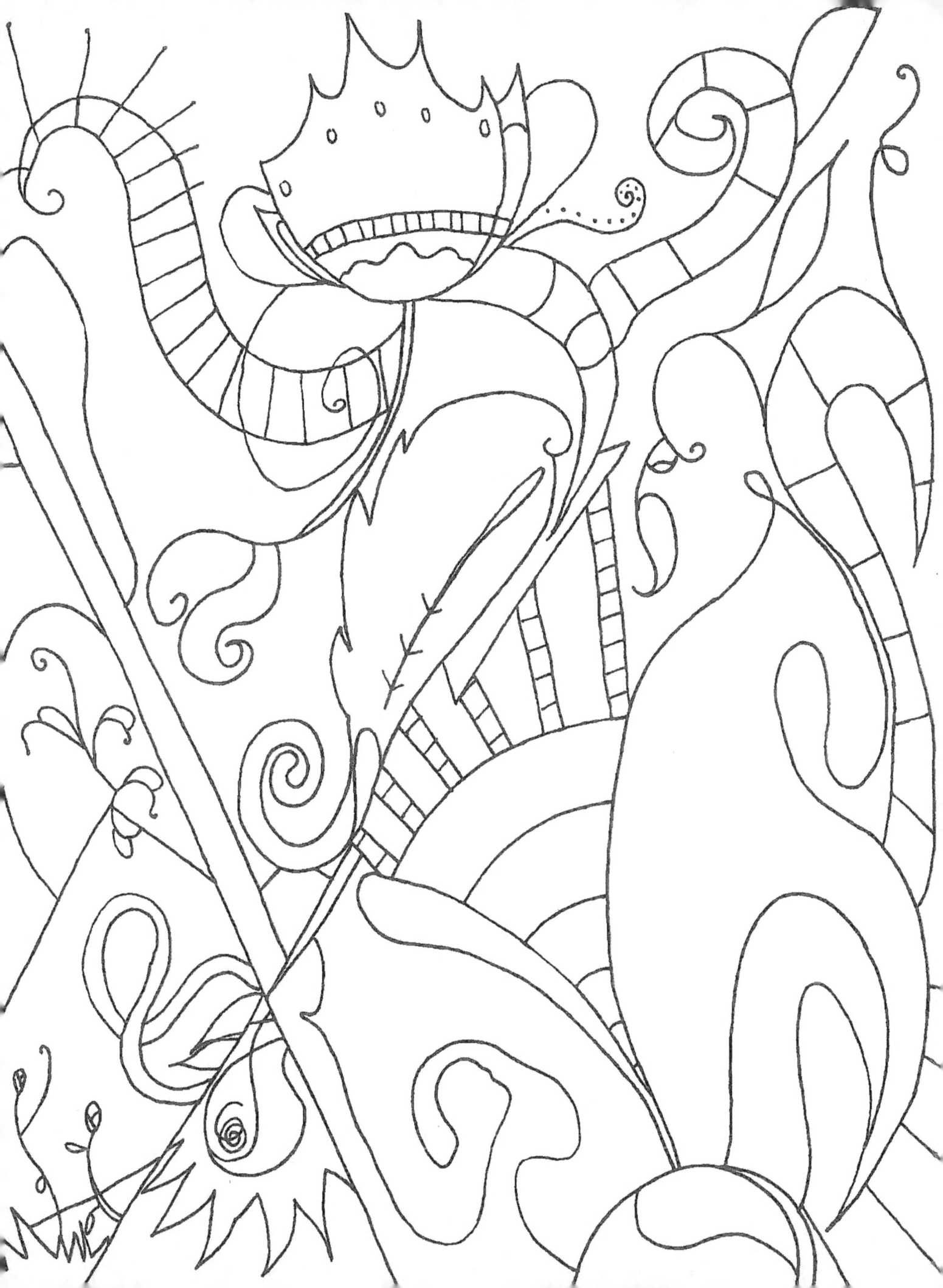

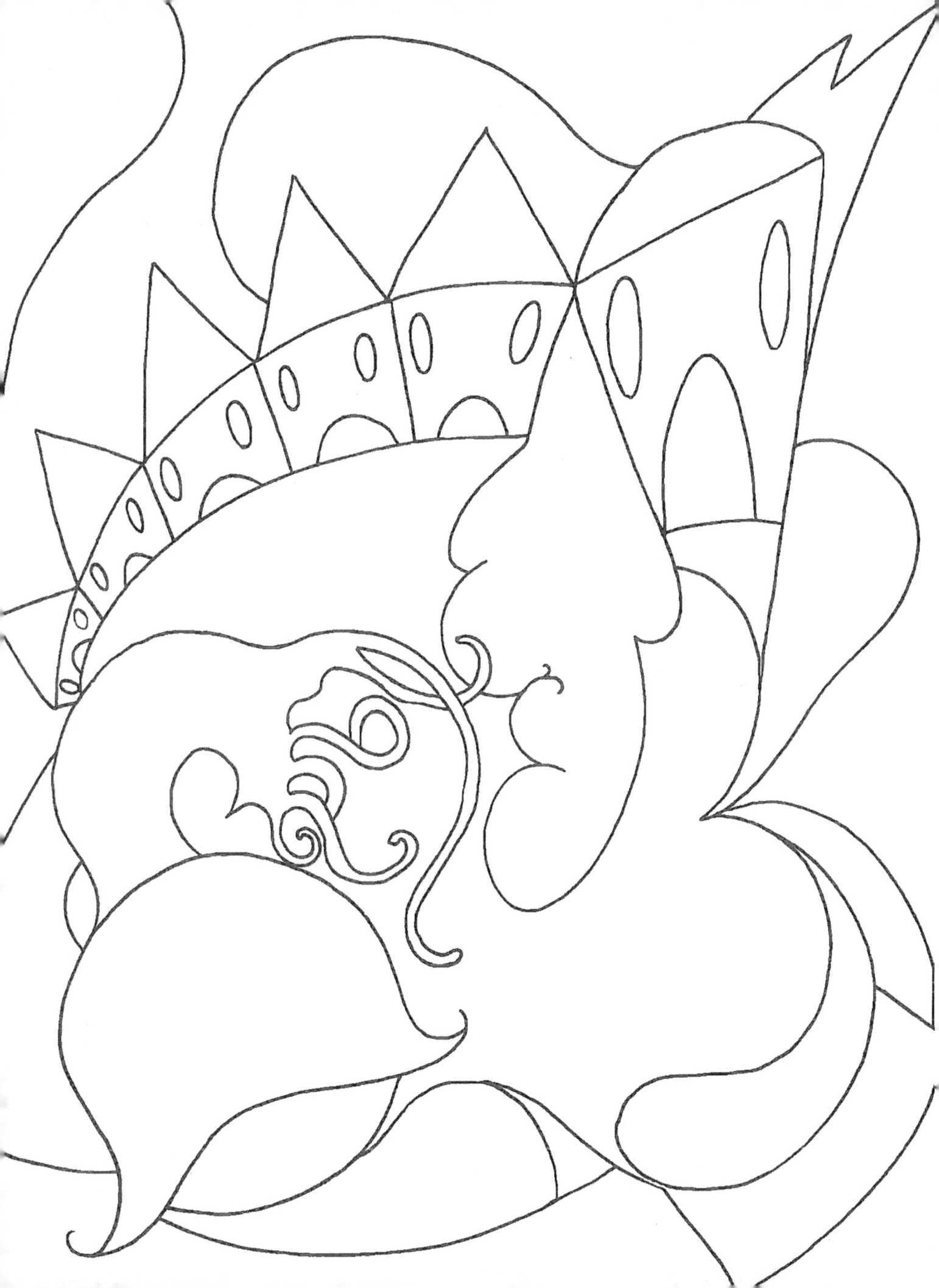

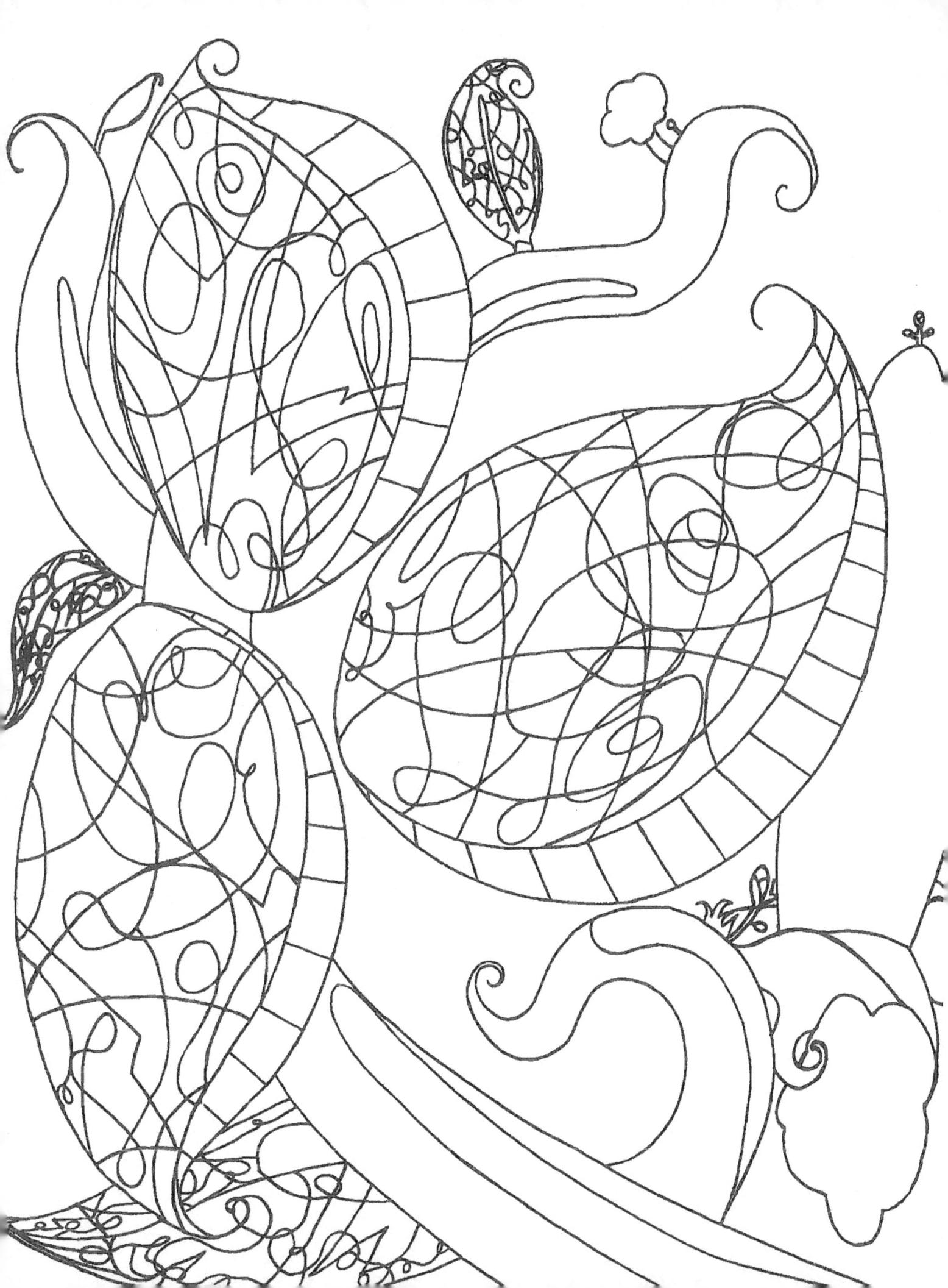

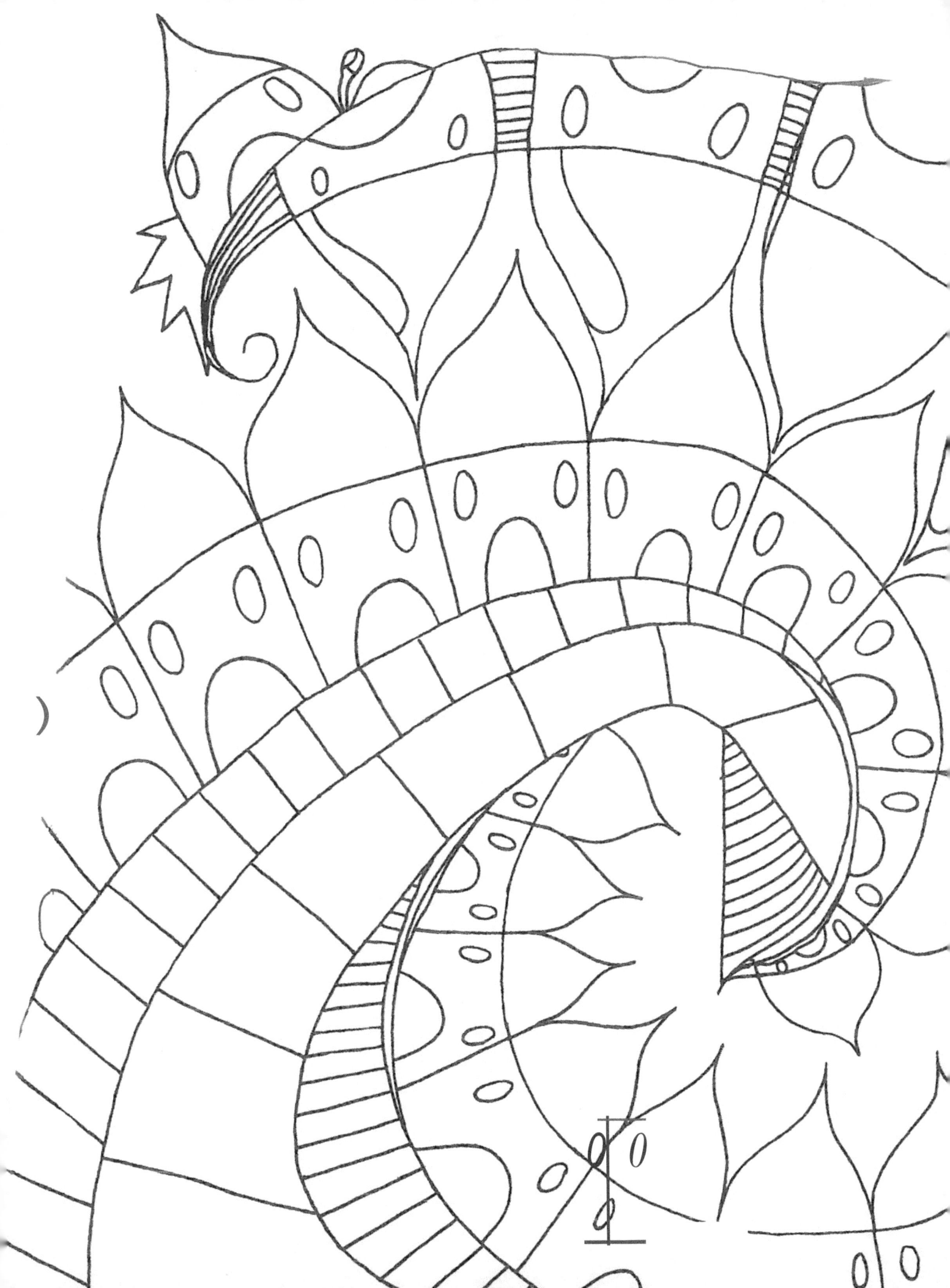

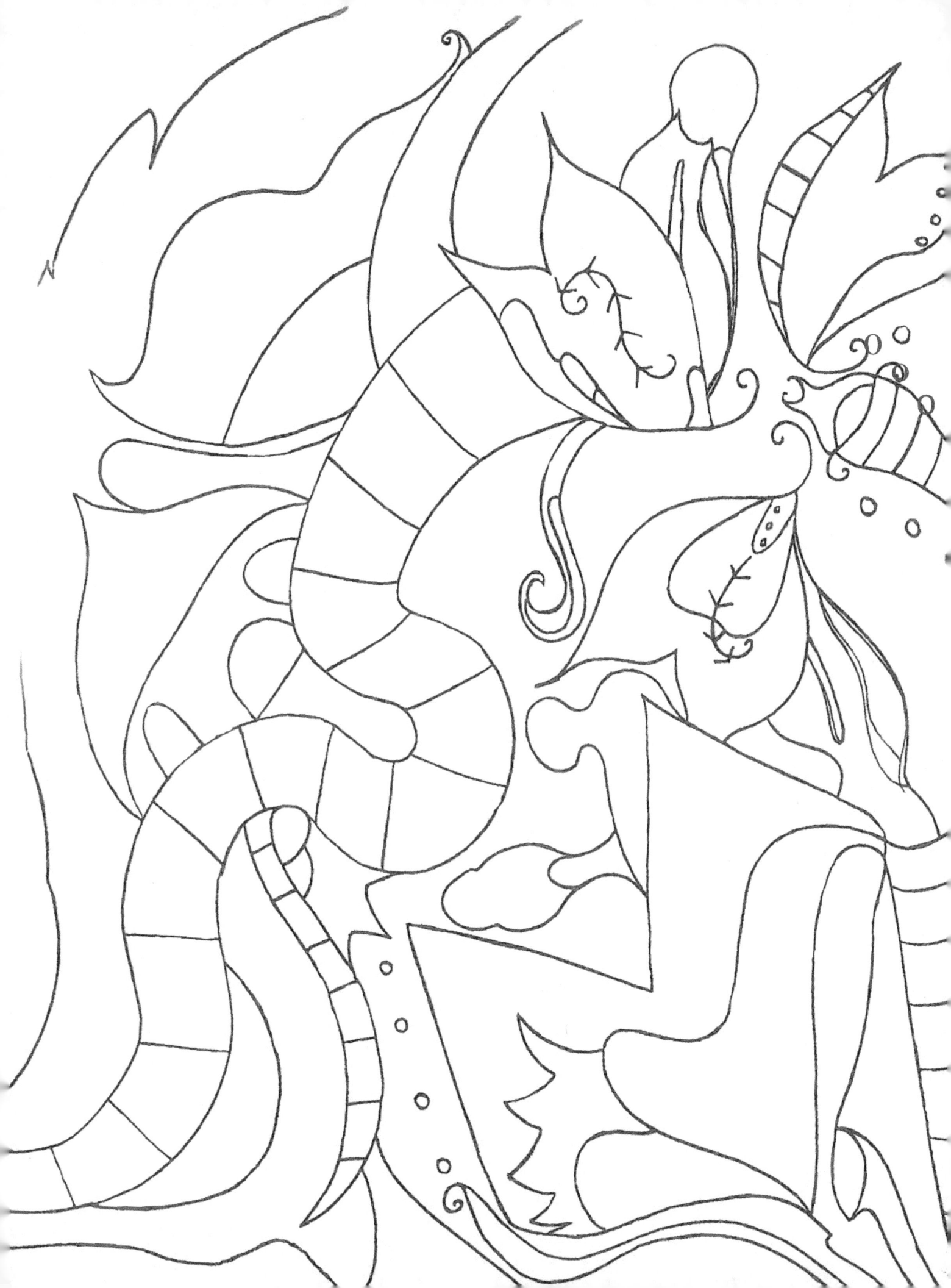

www.ingramcontent.com/pod-product-compliance
Lightning Source LLC
Chambersburg PA
CBHW080606180526
45168CB00007B/2803